[brief] guide **arte'm**

pompeii

edited by
massimo osanna
mario grimaldi
gabriel zuchtriegel

photographs by
pier paolo metelli

arte,m

coordinating editor
maria sapio

art director
enrica d'aguanno

translator
colum fordham

P O M P E I I

Soprintendenza Pompei
superintendent
Massimo Osanna

excavation director
Grete Stefani

MINISTERO
DEI BENI E
DELLE ATTIVITÀ
CULTURALI E
DEL TURISMO

arte'm
is a registered trademark
prismi
editrice politecnica napoli srl

quality
management system
ISO 9001: 2008
www.arte-m.net

printed in italy
© copyright 2016 by
soprintendenza pompei
prismi
editrice politecnica napoli srl
all rights reserved

printed
in july 2016

printing and layout
officine grafiche
francesco giannini
& figli spa, naples

MISTO
Carta da fonti gestite
in maniera responsabile
FSC® C124462

contents

introduction
massimo osanna

Within the ephemeral culture of show business, cultural heritage risks ending up in the maelstrom of special effects at all costs: in this scenario, 'masterpieces' are treated as 'attractions' and considered the only way of capturing the attention of the collective consciousness, or of competing with the status symbols of global society.

It is a paradigm that does not explain the success of Pompeii. Visitors from all over the world continue to flock in ever increasing numbers to the ancient city, to explore the ruins, precisely because of the potency of 'ordinary' life that still emanates from the city that re-emerged from the lava of Vesuvius, from the stories of everyday life that have left their traces in the homes, the shops and the sacred and profane public spaces.

It is arguably the vindication of history without clamour and rhetoric - the demonstration that it is possible to merit attention, stimulate curiosity and the critical imagination, renew values and roots, without eradicating the past and the magic vitality of the *genius loci* – the spirit of a place.

Tempus (time), life: this is the central theme that we have intentionally chosen for the new season of communication for the archaeological sites of the Vesuvian area.

With its inclusive identity, highly innovative multimedia displays and well-planned online promotion currently being developed, Pompeii is determined to offer the public 'tailor-made' access that goes beyond excessive specialisation, while maintaining the emphasis on rigorous, high quality research. In other words, it is possible to tell gripping stories precisely because of the capacity to continue investigating the roots and perspectives of our everyday lives.

This handy guide has been updated to include the new 'discoveries' of the permanent excavation site of the "Great Pompeii Project", which Gabriel Zuchtriegel and Mario Grimaldi now offer visitors from all cultural and geographical backgrounds. It is an integral part of the open mosaic of 'intelligent popularisation' designed to encourage new approaches that stimulate people's curiosity, participation and sustainable critical access.

on the previous page
View of the Forum

House of the Fruit Orchard
detail of the decoration

page 21
House of the Faun
Mosaic on the pavement
in front of the entrance

[in short]

A museum can be memorised rather artificially into a few 'unmissable masterpieces'. This does not help to understand stories, roots, passions and perspectives of works that encapsulate the dreams of a whole life, of many lives mixed up together. But at least it can convey the emotion of a sudden infatuation that can lead to more in-depth exploration.

However, this is not the case for Pompeii. The distinctive feature of the city lies precisely in its 'ordinary extraordinariness', in the eternal everyday life of two thousand years ago - the houses, the shops, the theatres, the forum, the gymnasia and the 'embalmed' bodies - as if time had stood still.

It is a treasure trove that cannot be appreciated in bite size chunks. It requires a gradual approach, an interior metabolism and the desire to interact..

The first 'piece of advice' for using this [brief] guide is therefore **to prepare the journey in advance**, to keep an eye on the wealth of material and multimedia information that add to the desire to visit the site each day - www.pompeisites.it , app ...

In technical terms, as regards 'practical' information, the **two suggested itineraries** offer **indications for getting one's bearings**. Beginning from the **Forum** – the hub of public life – the guide merely points out some of the most important sites moving **eastwards**, towards the **theatre** district, and **westwards**, to **Villa of the Mysteries**. Both itineraries require at least **2 hours** of careful exploration. Although inevitably skimming the surface, a **'complete' visit** would take not less than **4** hours, considerably more time than global tourism allows its 'clients'. The only thing that remains is to get rid of our preconceptions and explore the city at a leisurely pace with our hearts and minds. At the very least, if time is pressing, **you can prepare your visit both beforehand and afterwards** with curiosity and a keen sense of participation. Do try and **make a return visit**. It is an emotion, a 'story', that is worth far more than a casual visit.

what is pompeii?

a place frozen in time

In October 79 AD, after more than 800 years of inactivity, Vesuvius suddenly erupted. The power that had built up over the centuries destroyed the ancient crater, creating such an immense column of smoke and dust that the sky was plunged into darkness for three days. Ash and pumice – known as lapilli – 'rained down' over the entire area around the volcano: in a single day, the houses of cities like Pompeii and Herculaneum were submerged up to their roofs.

Few of the roughly 15,000 inhabitants managed to escape. Others sought refuge beneath roofs or

in cellars and were destined to die. On this day life in Pompeii came to a standstill. Loaves of bread stayed in the ovens, pots were left on stoves and money remained in safes. For over 1,600 years, everything remained intact. Shortly after the eruption, some people returned to the buried city in an attempt to recover precious objects, bronzes and marble: the general appearance of Pompeii was still recognisable and the roofs of houses and temples jutted out from the accumulated detritus. Only the areas of large public buildings such as the forum were plundered. The rest of the city fell into a deep sleep lasting well over a thousand years until the spring of 1748. Ten years previously, the excavations carried out at the site of Herculaneum had caused great excitement in the Kingdom of Naples and throughout Europe, prompting the search for the other large site whose existence was known but whose name remained a mystery: the city known by the Romans as Pompeii and by the Greeks as Pompeia. [g.z.]

the excavations

The settlement of Pompeii occupied an area of roughly 66 hectares, 44 of which have been brought to light. Two thirds of the city have therefore been revealed while a third still remains to be discovered. However, given the conservation problems facing the parts that have already been excavated – walls built 2000 years ago to last several generations have been exposed to the elements for up to two centuries – large scale excavations are no longer undertaken and attention is now focused on specific points to clarify the function and history of individual monuments.

The very first excavations, which began in 1748, used a system of shafts and underground galleries (known as 'cunicoli'). The walls were stripped of their frescoes which were installed in the museum built by the King of Naples. They can now be admired in the Archaeological Museum of Naples together with statues, furnishings and other objects unearthed during the excavations. Once the system of underground galleries had been abandoned, open air excavations were carried out. The commitment and energy devoted to exploring the site fluctuated according to the interests of the rulers of Naples. During the decade of French rule (1806-1815), Queen Carolina Bonaparte, wife of King Joachim Murat and sister of Napoleon, managed to recruit over 800 excavators.

During the nineteenth century the methodology of archaeological excavation made huge qualitative advances: archaeologists began to observe the stratigraphy and the sequence of the various natural and artificial sediments. One of the major innovators of stratigraphic excavation was Giuseppe Fiorelli, the director of the excavations from 1860 to 1875. The most

pages 22/23
Antiquarium
model of Pompeii

on the previous page
Basilica
detail of the columns
the Tribunal in the
background

Antiquarium
exedra of the pompeianists

Garden of the fugitives
Plaster casts of the bodies of
the victims of the eruption

page 31
Temple of Apollo

spectacular innovation was the technique of making plaster casts of the bodies of the victims. During the excavations empty spaces were sometimes discovered, often containing human bones. Fiorelli realised the reason and introduced a new procedure: the digging would stop and the empty space – the imprint left by a human body – was filled with plaster. This technique produced plaster casts of the bodies which had dissolved under the deluge of ash and lapilli from the eruption. After the Second World War, the excavations focused more systematically on the prehistory of Pompeii to study the evolution of the site over the centuries. [g.z.]

the history of the city

Pompeii was founded in the sixth century BC when small communities that had settled in the Sarno valley gradually merged, leading to the first phases of urbanisation. In Campania other Greek and Etruscan cities such as Paestum, Naples (known as Neapolis in Greek), Capua and Cuma were already flourishing. To keep up with these centres settlements had to be organised in a more structured way than small rural villages.

As early as the sixth century BC, Pompeii had city walls and religious sites (the Temple of Apollo and the Temple of Athena overlooking the triangular forum) where the community gathered for collective rituals.

Although Pompeii originated as an indigenous local settlement (inhabited by the Oscans who spoke an Indo-European language), archaeological evidence shows that there were frequent contacts with Greeks and Etruscans. The oldest inscriptions found in Pompeii are in Etruscan and the ruins of a large temple in the triangular forum resemble

contemporary Greek temples such as those at Paestum. The cult of the god Apollo, who was worshipped in the city forum, represents a Greek element in local culture.

In the fifth century BC Pompeii was occupied by another Italic people: the Samnites. Due in particular to its river port, the city continued to flourish even after the first clashes with the Romans who extended their power ever further south between the fourth and second century BC.

The second century BC was Pompeii's "golden age": many of the magnificent houses covered by the eruption of Vesuvius date to this period. The buildings dating to the second century BC can be recognised by the typical decoration of the First Style, such as those in the area around the entrance to the House of the Faun. After the social war between Rome and the Italic peoples (91-89 BC), the dictator Sulla founded a colony at Pompeii (80 BC).

Many of the old Samnite families disappeared. The city was populated with Roman veterans and some of them became the owners of ancient Samnite residences, restoring and refurbishing them (with decorations in the Second Style). The public sector of the city changed its appearance. The most important building during this phase was the amphitheatre but new buildings were also constructed such as baths and a roofed theatre (the small theatre). The temples were also restored.

An earthquake in 62 AD damaged many buildings in the city and the economy underwent a significant decline. At the time of the eruption in 79 AD, several prestigious residences had been converted to productive activities (as happened in the case of the Villa of the Mysteries): the Pompeii 'frozen in time' by Vesuvius was a provincial city whose period of greatest splendour belonged to the past. [*g.z.*]

the first style	the second style	the third style	the fourth style

The four Pompeian styles: four styles can be identified in the wall decoration of the houses of Pompeii. Identifying them makes it easy to date many of the monuments in the site. The First Style dates back to the Samnite period (3rd-2nd century BC) and is marked by pseudo-masonry in multi-coloured stucco. The Second Style (c.100-20 BC) is marked by the realistic representation of architecture, taken from theatre sets. The stucco relief decoration was also abandoned.

During the Third Style (c. 20 BC - 55/60 AD) the architectural features became increasingly abstract and ornamental; large monochrome panels painted in red and black with mythological scenes in the centre began to appear. The Fourth Style, which was in fashion when Pompeii was buried by ash, is the most widespread: the use of small mythological paintings continued and there was a return to less abstract, although often fanciful, forms of painted architecture on a white background. [g.z.]

legend

*the numbers in square brackets refer to the numbering system of the official site **map**; the number in black refers to the places mentioned in the **audio guide***

2

from the triangular forum to porta nocera

4 triangular forum [VIII.7, 8; **41**, **42**]
5 large theatre [VIII.10; **43**]
6 gladiators' barracks [VIII.11; **44**]
7 odeion [VIII.12; **45**]
8 house of menander [I.7; **51**]
9 house of the cryptoporticus [I.5]
10 fullonica of stephanus [I.3; **52**]
11 house of paquius proculus [I.8]
12 house of the ephebe [I.9]
13 house of giulius polibius [IX.4; **54**]
14 house of the orchard [I.11]
15 house of octavius quartius [II.1; **58**]
16 house of venus in the shell [II.2; **59**]
17 amphitheatre [II.5; **60**]
18 large palaestra [II.6; **61**]
19 fortifications and cemetery of porta nocera [II.9, 10; **62**, **63**]
20 garden of the fugitives [I.14; **56**]

from porta marina
to the civic forum

1 porta marina

The entrance to Pompeii through Porta Marina, one of the seven gateways of the city, involves a steep climb up from the ancient level of the river Sarno, which passed beneath the city walls, to the rocky spur on which the city stands. The highest part behind Porta Marina was the site of the heart of the city containing the Forum and the main temples (the Temple of Apollo, the Temple of Venus, the Temple of Jupiter overlooking the Forum and the Temple of Athena in the so-called Triangular Forum). The residential districts are situated beyond the Forum as far as the area of the Amphitheatre on the other side of the city.

Modern archaeologists have divided the urban area into nine regions, each of which is subdivided into blocks (*insulae*) with a number for each house. These numbers, found on many of the houses, are therefore a modern addition. The inhabitants had other names for various zones of the city which are only partly known. For example, the original name of Porta Marina was *Porta Forensis* since it was the gate of the Forum district. [*g.z.*]

Stabian baths

Porta Marina

2 antiquarium and the imperial villa

The area of Porta Marina was affected by major restoration work and excavations related to the renovation of the Antiquarium which was partly destroyed by bombardment during the Second World War.

The new museum building was erected in 1947 and overlay the plan of the previous structure promoted by Fiorelli. On this occasion Maiuri explored the underlying levels containing the lower rooms of the villa. He discovered the first evidence for rooms and cisterns belonging to the villa which were discovered beneath the floor level of the Antiquarium.

As well as cisterns, several buttresses situated on the western side behind the line of the limestone walls were found. In his notes, Maiuri also mentioned the discovery, on the upper square, of masonry structures related to the villa although this was not confirmed by the excavations carried out in 1984.

The recent restoration of the Antiquarium, which is finally due to re-open, has made it possible to investigate the following aspects:
- the relationship between the plans of the lower floor and the upper floor of the villa;
- its relationship with the complex system of cisterns found here;
- its relationship with the area of the Temple of Venus;
- the possible relationships with the large so-called granary complex.

By looking at the excavation photos, it immediately becomes apparent that over half the current building was reconstructed by Amedeo Maiuri. Indeed the archive photos reveal a complex that had been almost completely destroyed at the time of the eruption. This is confirmed by the notes in the excavation diaries where explicit mention is made of a large layer of deposit (about 3 metres thick) consisting of the rubble from the upper part of the building and the waste that accumulated over a very long period. A layer of lapilli from the eruption of 79 AD which had sealed the deposit was found above it.

The restoration work of 1948 therefore altered the appearance of the area shortly before the eruption since while the granaries were being built, the villa must have looked like a disused ruin which had largely been destroyed.

The imperial villa, decorated in the Third and Fourth Styles, was only destroyed by the earthquake of 62 AD. At the time of the eruption it had already been abandoned and looted for over a decade (indeed, all the floors made of *opus sectile* were missing).

It is therefore no coincidence that the Granary complex had been located in this area without any regard for the luxurious rooms that had previously existed. Indeed, the excavation photos suggest that the Granaries were newly constructed and overlay the Imperial Villa, a ruin that had long been abandoned.

From the moment of its completion, the Imperial Villa complex was linked to the destiny of the south-western corner of the city.

on the previous pages
Antiquarium
entrance

Imperial Villa
main reception room with decoration in
Third-Fourth Style

Its location close to the limestone city walls and its position below the terrace of the Temple of Venus shed light on our understanding of the urban development of Pompeii on this side.

The research carried out in front of the Antiquarium area of Pompeii should be interpreted within this context.

Proceeding in chronological order, the line of the limestone wall of the Sarno, which dates to the first Samnite phase (4th-3rd century BC) is the oldest feature, built as a means of fortification and containment of the fill between the terrace of the temple and the western line.

Buttresses 1-8 were built in close correspondence with the walls, following the pattern of the fortifications both in terms of their plan and their depth. Judging from their stratigraphic relationship with the walls, already noted by Mauri in the 1947 excavations, they do not appear to have been a substructure of the fortifications. This is because their trapezoid arrangement and their position within the defensive line seem to be related mainly to the need to discharge weight onto the walls. They must have been intended to provide support for rooms that could not be built directly on the area and on the walls. Proof of this is provided by the physical relationship between USMs 5, 6, and 7 (masonry stratigraphic units), partition walls that point to the existence of a large room, and buttresses 7 and 8 to which they are directly linked in planimetric terms, taking account of construction levels.

Another distinctive feature of the area is the large cistern complex, oriented north-east-south-west like the villa, which appears to have been designed to drain water along this side. The roof vaults of the cisterns, situated at a lower level (c. 4.00 metres below ground level), had been destroyed and filled with waste material, identical to the material found over the whole area, for the construction on the west side of barrel vaults belonging to the large "granary" building constructed on the southern side of the city below the Temple of Venus.

The plan of the villa, with cisterns in a raised central area, rooms to the west overlooking panoramic terraces and a large *xystus* (long portico) in the lower level, displays typological parallels with the large luxurious villas with walkways (*villas ad ambulation*) on Capri (Villa Jovis, Damecuta) and Baïae and Miseno (the so-called Caesar's Villa, Villa of Punta Epitaffio). Examples of highly sophisticated Third Style decoration dating to the Augustan Age are preserved such as the *Cycle of Theseus and the Minotaur* which can be seen in the main room overlooking the large colonnade. The high quality of the work is also shown by the desire of the painter to give the names of the illustrated characters in Greek (still visible on the south wall). [m.g.]

Imperial Villa
Theseus and the minotaur
main reception room east wall
Nymph
Main reception room south wall

on the following pages
View of the civic forum
east side

on page 47
Building of Eumachia
(Porticus Concordiae)

3 civic forum

The civic forum is situated in the centre of Pompeii and, as building development continued, became the hub of everyday life in the city and political events.

The oldest evidence for the area consists of the Temple of Apollo which, from the sixth century BC, overlooked an open space through its eastern side made up of six entrances, some of which were sealed during subsequent renovation work on the building during the Samnite period.

The Forum was originally just a roughly regular area of compacted earth with the Temple of Apollo on the western side and a row of *tabernae*, fitted with poles and awnings, on the eastern side. The new layout, dating to the second century BC, featured a rectangular area paved with tuff slabs, entirely surrounded by a colonnade. The longitudinal axis focuses on the façade of the Temple of Jupiter, situated in line with *Mons Vesuvius*, now known simply as Vesuvius.

The Basilica (130-120 BC), which occupied an area of 1500 square metres, was the most magnificent building in the Forum during this phase. Built directly along the street that led to the river port (Via Marina), it acted as the centre for the administration of justice and for commerce. The building, with three naves, was constructed by a highly skilled architect and an excellent workshop. Its role as the financial and commercial centre gave the highly ornate tribune specific functions, such as the podium for auctions. The entrance to the Basilica originally looked out directly onto the forum like the other public buildings. Following the construction of the *Comitium* and the Basilica, it became necessary to regulate this side of the forum. This prompted the duumvirs, or rather the

quaestors (*quaestores*), to build a portico in front of these buildings to bring order to the original layout marked by a lack of alignment. The long eastern side, apart for the *Macellum*, remained without any representative structures and was occupied solely by *tabernae*. The Samnite layout of the Forum therefore lacked a unified political strategy which does appear, at least initially, in the transformation and construction of economic and commercial buildings such as the *Macellum* and the Basilica. During the pre-colonial period, buildings such as the Temple of Jupiter, the so-called *Comitium* and administrative buildings symbolised the will of Pompeii's citizens to obtain full Roman citizenship which they had long sought although their request had been obstinately rejected by the Senate. The second phase in the development of the city began when Pompeii was made a colony (*Colonia Cornelia Veneria Pompeianorum*)in 80 BC.

The *Comitium*, which was begun in the Hellenistic period, was completed and its original function as a polling station changed to become a vote counting office (*Diribitorium*), while the Forum was used for voting, based on the model of other Roman colonies.

The leading magistrates had honorary statues erected on large bases opposite the administrative buildings. The most conspicuous change was the transformation of the Temple of Jupiter into the *Capitolium*, dating to the initial phase of the colony. The new building stood on an ancient podium in the Italic style. The *cella* (the inner area of the temple) was lengthened and it became a two-storey building with columns, mosaic floors and Second Style paintings. The original grand central staircase was replaced by two lateral staircases. The three cult statues were arranged within the *cella* inside a shrine with a high podium.

A new altar was built in honour of Apollo, the ancient deity of the city, by the new ruling class made up of *duumvirs* and *aediles*.

A third period of construction dates to the early phase of the Empire in the late first century BC and the early first century AD. Almost all the public building during this period began from 20 BC onwards, immediately after the creation of the Principate by Augustus.

Priesthoods therefore played an extremely important role. The Temple of Apollo was held in new regard since Augustus' protective deity was Apollo, the god who helped him defeat Mark Anthony at Actium in 31 BC. This explains the importance of the *Ludi Apollinares*, the games held in his honour which took place at the time

The proclamation of *pietas* prevented Augustus from allowing his own cult. His *genius* could only be worshipped together with the other Lares but he had no objection if the deities, or the personification of the Virtues currently in vogue, were given the title *Augustus*. An example is the construction of the new Temple of Fortuna Augusta by *M. Tullius*, situated outside the Civic Forum but at one of the most important crossroads of the city. The old shops (*tabernae*) on the eastern side of the Forum were demolished to make way for two new buildings designed for the Imperial cult: the Temple of the Public Lares and the Temple of the *Genius Augusti*.

The Temple of the Public Lares preceded the earthquake of 62 AD but was built after the Augustan Principate. The elaborate marble decoration, which was missing at the time of the discovery of Pompeii, was plundered during the long period when the first excavations were carried out at forum after the eruption of 79 AD.

The unusual building marks the boundary of an unroofed area. To the sides of the apsidal areas, the building, which overlooked the Forum, has two large rectangular exhedras and numerous niches destined for statues of members of the imperial family. In the centre of the building there was an altar where the emperor could also be worshipped as the *Genius Augusti*.

To the right of the *Lararium*, the Temple of the *Genius Augusti* was built in the Augustan period by Mamia, as can be seen from the niche motifs on the façade, resembling those of Eumachia's building, and from the altar which was restored and partly completed after 62 AD. It included a small religious area with an open space in front of it, an altar and a tetrastyle shrine on a high podium which was accessible from two sides. Another public priestess (Eumachia, *sacerdos publica*) commissioned the most imposing building on the eastern side of the Forum. She wanted to dedicate the building to the *Concordia Augusta* and to *Pietas*. The dedication also includes the name of her son *M. Numistrius Fronto*, who can be identified as the *duumvir* of 2-3 AD, with clear propaganda purposes for the family.

As mentioned in the inscription placed above the columns of the façade, to which a second order of Ionic columns was added, the building combines various features: *chalcidicum, crypta* and *porticus*. Travertine was used as the building material.

The *chalcidicum* is the large vestibule that corresponds to the portico with a double nave at the entrance. The short southern side was closed by a metal gate and a statue base; the founder therefore forced visitors to enter from the side of the main façade.

The two inscriptions that were discovered describe the figures of Romulus and Aeneas (*elogia*) placed beneath the small niches on the outer walls to the sides of the apsidal exhedras. They refer to the iconographic and epigraphic programme of illustrious men (*summi viri*) in the Forum of Augustus. The two rectangular exhedras to the sides were faced in marble and were used for delivering speeches on imperial feast-days. The long series of bases for statues, placed against the inner side of the columns, gave the *chalcidicum* a dignified character and it would have contained a gallery of honorary statues of eminent figures.

The interior consisted of a portico with three wings which, on the short eastern side, opened onto two small semi-circular exhedras on the sides of the niche for the cult of the *Concordia Augusta*. A statue would have originally been placed inside the niche and it has recently been identified as a *Pietas with* cornucopia, now kept in the Archaeological Museum in Naples. Behind the portico was the crypt (*crypta*), also with three wings, in the centre of which stood the statue of Eumachia, the direct emanation of the *Concordia Augusta*. From the crypt there was a view of the small gardens situated behind the cult niche. The slave market (*venalicium*) may have taken place within this building.

Due to a previously existing street, the *Macellum* was situated obliquely with respect to the square and had not changed its appearance since Hellenistic times. The layout, which had a simpler plan without a *tholos* (130-120 BC), occupied roughly the same area as the Augustan building. In its new guise with a *tholos* (a round building), it also had a cult area in an elevated position, built on the eastern side, in line with the entrance. To its left there was a building where meetings of a religious college were held, while on the right there were fishmongers shops protected by the river Sarno which was once visible in the wall decoration in the Fourth Style. The two statues found in the niches to the right portrayed members of the imperial family.

During the third phase four splendid new buildings were constructed on the short eastern side of the Forum. All dedicated in various ways to the imperial cult, they were funded by private individuals. Apparently, there were no restrictions that prevented the façades of new buildings from protruding at an irregular angle into the public square. The eastern side had a series of private vestibules rather than a continuous portico.

The square took on a completely new appearance during the early imperial age. Large equestrian statues, whose presence can be inferred from the pedestals on the western side and in front of the administrative buildings, began to be built after Pompeii became a colony. During the Augustan age, some of the statues placed on the southern side of the square had to be removed to make way for an arched monument. Inspired by the famous model of the forum of Augustus in Rome, the arch may have been surmounted by the chariot of the *pater patriae*.

On either side of the arch two large monuments– possibly two colossal equestrian statues – were erected and placed on large square pedestals in line with the square.

The long western side was used for less important statues, possibly of local notables, partly standing figures (*pedestres*) and partly equestrian figures (*equestres*).

The short northern side had two honorary arches of imperial princes on either side of the *Capitolium*. The right-hand arch, possibly dedicated to Germanicus or Nero, was moved further back or demolished until as far as the street to give prominence to the new façade of the vestibule of the *Macellum* and to provide an improved visual link between the Temple of *Fortuna Augusta* and the portico leading to it. The left-hand arch was probably dedicated to Drusus.

To the sides of the *Capitolium* there were two equestrian statues, as can be seen in the relief on the lararium of L. Cecilius Giocondus which portrays the *Capitolium*.

Macellum
Detail of the Fourth Style decoration
West wall

During the early years of the imperial period, the Forum was re-paved with travertine slabs, replacing the tuff slabs used during the Samnite phase. A bronze inscription, of which only a few letters remain, ran along the paving slabs in the place where political

orations were delivered (*suggestum*); the inscription mentioned the name of the donor. The plinth was probably an altar for the imperial cult, surrounded on three sides by imperial honorary monuments. Its alignment with the cult buildings suggests a sort of new orientation of the Forum towards the newly constructed public buildings. [*m.g.*]

Exterior of the Macellum
and colonnade of the Forum

Temple of Apollo
Altar and sundial

from the stabian baths
to the villa of the mysteries

4 stabian baths

The Stabian baths are renowned in Roman archaeology for their antiquity and excellent state of preservation (some rooms still have their original ceilings). The structures reveal the development of Roman baths from simple bathing pools in the Hellenistic period (3rd century BC) to splendid imperial baths (1st century AD) provided with an ingenious heating system.

Via dell'Abbondanza leads to a large courtyard with a colonnade on three sides: this is the *palaestra* (the word deriving from a Greek term), an area for athletics training.

The baths developed from the pools that were an integral part of these spaces: over time the public baths became more important than gymnastic activities. On the left-hand side there is a complex decorated in stucco (Augustan age, c.31 BC-14 AD) and a cold water swimming pool (*natatio*), while the actual baths begin to the right of the colonnade. The first entrance leads through the changing rooms (*apodyterium*) to the men's area which was larger and more elaborately decorated than the women's section. The heating system can be seen in the indoor rooms. Double floors and terracotta pipes in the walls enabled the hot air from the *praefurnium*, the hidden furnace

tended by a slave, to spread through the building and heat it with the additional support of bronze braziers during winter. The baths were arranged according to the temperature of the water. The *apodyterium* is followed by the *tepidarium*, a bath with warmer water. To the left there is a circular room called the *frigidarium* for plunging into cold water while opposite there is the *calidarium* for hot baths.

Access to the women's baths, which have a similar arrangement to the men's baths but lack a *frigidarium*, was from via Lupanare (as indicated by the word *Mulier* – women – painted on the entrance, although the writing has now disappeared). [g.z.]

on the previous pages
Vestibule
Detail of the ceiling in
Fourth Style

Entrance to the Baths

Portico

Men's tepidarium
suspensurae (false floors)
and *pilae* (brick piers) for
hypocaust heating system

on the following pages
Vestibule

Women's caldarium

5 brothel (lupanar)

This is one of the areas of the city devoted to prostitution. In most cases they are individual rooms added onto a shop (*taberna*) or part of a house (as in the House of the Vettii). However, in the brothel the opportunity to earn money from forced prostitution (mainly female slaves but also male slaves judging from Pompeian inscriptions and ancient texts) was exploited to the utmost by rationalising space as far as possible. Along the corridor linking the two entrances on the ground floor there are five rooms, each with a stone bed and a latrine, closed off by curtains for which bronze rings have been found. The small paintings with erotic themes on the walls of the central corridor were intended to 'encourage' the desires and fantasies of clients and employ widespread figurative layouts also found in the House of the Vettii and the suburban Baths below Porta Marina. A third entrance leads, through a small room with a latrine, to an upper floor which has been partly reconstructed in modern times. The balcony running along the two outer sides of the building provided access to five rooms of varying size which may have been the residences of female slaves and the brothel-owner. [*g.z.*]

Interior

erotic paintings
entrance to the alcove

6 house of the faun

This is the largest and wealthiest house in Pompeii and occupies a block of about 3,000 square metres. Access is not through an entrance area (*vestibulum* and *fauces* in Latin) but through one of the shops to the side on via della Fortuna where the owner's commercial activities took place or which were rented to small shopkeepers or artisans. The exquisite decoration of the entrance, which is visible from the outside, cannot cope with the continuous flow of visitors. The floor is made up of triangular stones of various colours *(opus sectile)*. The wall decoration in the First Style, with models of shrines on both sides, dates to the second century BC when the house took on the appearance it maintained until the eruption of 79 AD. The pavement in front of the large door, which has two pilasters with stone capitals (2nd century BC), bears an inscription of welcome: the Latin greeting *have*.

Like the entrance, the interior of the house contains evidence of First Style paintings (3rd-2nd century BC). At the centre of the atrium - a kind of foyer - there is an *impluvium*, a rectangular pool that collected rainwater through an opening in the roof (the *compluvium*). The

of a bomb can be seen in the south-east corner. The bomb was dropped as part of the bombardment of Pompeii in August and September 1943 during the Allied landings (a German gun emplacement was thought to be on the site).

The area behind the house consists of two large peristyles - courtyards with plants and flowers, surrounded by colonnades - with the remains of First Style wall decoration. The famous mosaic of *Darius and Alexander*, portraying the battle of Alexander the Great with the Persian king Darius, was discovered in a communicating room between the first and the second peristyle (no. 37) in the years 1829-33. The site contains a copy while the original mosaic is in the Archaeological Museum of Naples. [*g.z.*]

pool is decorated with a bronze sculpture of the *Faun* (actually the god Pan), now in the Archaeological Museum of Naples, which gave the house its name.

On the two sides of the *atrium* there are a series of small rooms (*cubicula*, bedrooms or sitting rooms), while at the back there is the *tablinum*, the study where the owner met his clients and friends to discuss business and politics. The atrium leads to a second atrium (room 7) where the fragments

on the previous pages
Statue of the Faun

Tablinum

Lararium
decoration in First Style

Impluvium with the statue
of the Faun

on the following pages
copy of the mosaic of the
Battle of Alexander

7 house of the vettii

Together with House of the Faun, the House of the Vettii is the most famous house in Pompeii although it is extremely different: instead of First Style decoration, this house has one of the most extraordinary series of Fourth Style frescoes (c.55 - 79 AD) with a rich iconographic programme of mythological themes and figures. The entrance is watched over by the figure of *Priapus* (the painting

to the right of the door) whose enormous member symbolises the economic prosperity of the owners, the brothers Aulus Vettius Restitutus and Aulus Vettius Conviva, whose wealth derived from commerce in wine and agricultural produce.

The house lacks a *tablinum*, the traditional reception room and study usually situated in the atrium opposite the entrance, which was sacrificed to create more space for the large peristyle. The most elaborately decorated

on the previous pages
Room of the Erotes
Decoration in the
Fourth Style

Frieze with cupids
detail

Ithyphallic Priapus
Door to the right of the
entrance

rooms overlook the peristyle and contain a series of refined mythological paintings designed to reflect the owners' elevated cultural status.

The themes illustrated in the paintings include the following: *Hercules as a child strangling the serpents* sent by the jealous goddess Juno (room n, wall N), *Daedalus presenting the wooden cow to Pasiphae*, mother of the Minotaur (room p, on the left), the *Punishment of Ixion* who was bound to the wheel for trying to seduce Juno (room n, central wall) and *Dionysus discovering the sleeping Ariadne*, abandoned by Theseus on the island of Naxos (room n, on the right).

The ancillary rooms are more modest and

smaller, such as the kitchen (room w) which leads to the small room (x) decorated with erotic pictures similar to the ones in the Brothel. Their presence here suggests that the slave girl Eutychis, "offered" for two asses according to a painted inscription on the outer walls of the house, was forced to prostitute herself to contribute to the wealth of the owners. [*g.z.*]

Room with the infant Hercules strangling snakes and the Punishment of Ixion Decoration in Fourth Style

8 house of the tragic poet

This medium-sized mansion is renowned for its magnificent decoration in the Fourth Style (c. 55 - 79 AD). It generally preserves the traditional layout of the atrium house, the traditional Etruscan-Roman house that emerged from the fifth century BC onwards. The main entrance was on via Mercurio and has the famous mosaic with the words *cave canem* ("beware of the dog").

On the two sides there are a series of shops and taverns that do not communicate with the house and were probably rented.

For conservation reasons, access is from a side entrance which leads directly into the garden with the colonnade on three sides. From the garden there is a splendid view of the *tablinum* where the owner received clients and the atrium with bedrooms to the side *(cubicula)*.

The *Tablinum* and *atrium* were decorated with elegant mosaics including the theatre scene that lends its name to the house. To prevent slaves passing through the *tablinum* when guests were present, a small side corridor made it possible to move from the atrium to the rear of the house. Special attention was paid to the decoration of the large room that looked onto the garden: the mythological paintings show *Ariadne abandoned by Theseus on the Island of Naxos*, the *Sale of the Cupids* and *Artemis with Callisto*, the nymph who was the companion of the goddess Artemis. As a punishment for getting pregnant, she was turned into a bear by

on the previous pages
Atrium

Cave canem
Mosaic at the entrance

Ariadne abandoned by
Theseus on the island of
Naxos
Detail of the decoration of
the room to the east of the
peristyle

on the following pages
View of the lararium

the goddess and later into a constellation (Ursa Major) by Zeus.

There is a small shrine at the back of the peristyle, next to the secondary side entrance: this is the *lararium*, a feature of virtually all the houses in Pompeii, which was dedicated to the daily worship of the Lares and other deities that protected the family. Due to its excellent state of preservation, the House of the Tragic Poet, excavated in 1824-25, is one of the most famous houses in Pompeii. It provided the setting for part of Edward Bulwer-Lytton's novel *The Last Days of Pompeii* (1838). [g.z.]

face monuments (known as *monumenta* in Latin) became increasingly large and elaborate while the grave goods of underground burials (*sepulcra*) were less prestigious in appearance. The ruling class built funerary shrines which were based on religious architecture linked to the worship of deities and heroes.

Leaving Porta Ercolano, there are two monuments on the right that consist of semi-circular benches made of tuff. This type of monument is typical of Pompeii and also appears in several temples (for example, in the Triangular Forum). They were known as *schola* (from the Greek term *schole*, "leisure", the root of the word 'school'), and referred to a meeting place.

The second *schola* monument on the southern side of the street has an inscription in large lettering on the back which gives the name of the tomb's owner: *Mamia*, the public priestess (who died in about 29 AD) who built the Temple of the Genius of Augustus in the Forum. Mamia's tomb was located in one of the first areas of the site to be excavated and had a major impact on illustrious visitors from the eighteenth century onwards, such as Goethe and Anna Amalia, Duchess of Weimar. The duchess had her portrait painted by Goethe's friend the artist Johann H.W. Tischbein and is shown seated on a bench of the *schola* type.

Behind the tomb, there are the ruins of a round shrine with Ionic columns (distinguished by the capitals with volutes or scrolls), built on a rectangular podium. This

9 the cemetery of porta ercolano

The cemetery of Porta Ercolano is situated along the street that led to Naples and Rome. During the Samnite period (4th-2nd century BC) the more prestigious tombs consisted of coffins with pottery and metal objects (weapons and jewellery). In some cases, there were monuments on the surface such as the sculpture of a stone sphinx (now lost). From the first century BC onwards, the sur-

is the funerary monument of the *Istacidii*, an eminent family in Pompeii who also owned the Villa of the Mysteries, situated further on along the street leading from Porta Ercolano.

Shortly afterwards, there is a niche tomb to the right with another semi-circular bench inside. The building has the form of a *nymphaeum*, a shrine dedicated to nymphs inspired by a natural cave, and this aspect is reinforced by the Fourth Style decoration (shells, blue background on the inside). The façade is decorated in stucco and resembles a work of religious architecture with two Corinthian columns and a pediment with a cornice. The centre of the pediment has a slab intended for the name of the deceased. However, the space remains empty because the tomb was probably never used as it had been built just before the eruption of 79 AD. [*g.z.*]

Funerary monument
of the Istacidii family

'niche' tomb

The construction of the villa – the term used by the Romans to describe a rural complex with agricultural and/or residential functions – dates to the second century BC. However, it was after 80 BC, when Sulla's colonists-veterans arrived in the city, that the building acquired its current appearance, probably following a change of ownership, including the famous Second Style decorations. In terms of size and quality, the wall decorations are without parallel in the whole of Pompeii.

In antiquity, access was through a courtyard-garden (peristyle) rather than through the atrium as in urban houses. The entrance area has never been excavated so that access is through one of the side rooms devoted to processing and storing agricultural produce. This leads to a terrace-substructure with arches on which the most representative rooms of the complex are situated. At the centre there is an atrium whose roof was reconstructed in the modern era, surrounded by rooms of various size decorated with exquisite frescoes. The series of rooms culminates in an exhedra (no. 1) overlooking the sea from where there would once have been a splendid view of the Sorrento peninsula and Capri. The large room (no.5) that gave the villa its name is especially interesting. The walls are decorated with a frieze that runs around the room, from the left as you enter, and is one of the largest and most beautiful paintings known from

antiquity. Although archaeologists have not managed to decipher all the features in the frieze, the frescoes undoubtedly depict scenes from the mysteries. Associated with several deities – in this case Dionysus who appears on the central wall with Ariadne – This was the mysteries involved rituals in which only initiates (*mystai* in Greek) could

mysteries of Bacchus, which were initially performed exclusively by women (men were only admitted subsequently), had become a source of alarm which even posed a threat to public order.

The frieze of the mysteries is organised into a series of scenes that portray female figures involved in ritual activities and mythological figures (fauns, maenads and winged figures). As well as dancing and the consumption of wine, linked to the Dionysian trance, the frieze shows the ritual flagellation of a girl, seated on the lap of a seated woman, by a winged female demon.

Although it is part of the most representative complex of the villa, the room of the mysteries is set back from the main entrance, located on the other side of the building, so that access to the room could be restricted to a privileged and select circle of friends and guests. [g.z.]

participate. Anyone who had been initiated in the cult of the mysteries was forbidden from describing what happened during the ritual celebrations which explains why so little is known about these cults from the written sources. In 186 BC the Roman Senate issued a decree against the mysteries linked to Dionysus-Bacchus (*Senatus consultum de Bacchanalibus*) which were alleged to have encouraged depravity through orgies and horrific rituals. The sources describe how the

on page 80
Cubicle
Detail of the Second Style decoration

on page 81
Mysteries room
Megalography
west wall
Detail of the Second Style decoration

on the previous pages
Mysteries room
Megalography
North and south walls
Detail of the Second Style
decoration

Mysteries room
Megalography
North wall
Detail of the Second Style
decoration

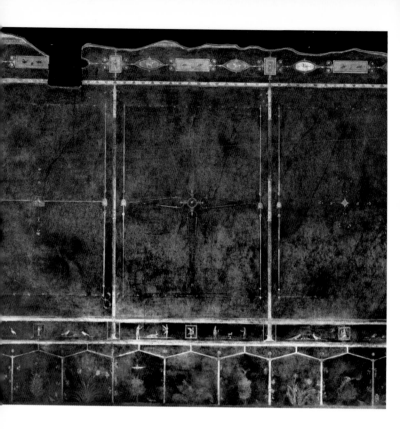

from the triangular forum
to porta nocera

4 triangular forum

The Triangular Forum, which owes its name to its geometric layout, stands on the spur of lava which dominates the Pompeian countryside to the south. The monumental façade on Via dei Teatri leads to a vestibule with six Ionic columns, preceded by a public fountain, and to the larger inner portico (2nd century BC) with 95 Doric columns built of tuff surrounding the area of the Doric Temple (6th century BC). The temple is built on a podium that rests directly on the spur of lava and was dedicated to Athena, Hercules and later to Minerva . It was restored several times between the sixth and the second century BC. The cella, enclosed by a colonnade (peristasis) of the Doric order, contained a double plinth designed for two cult statues: the statue of Athena, protectress of sailors (the promontory of Punta della Campanella near Sorrento, the site of an important temple of Athena, was visible from the terrace of the temple) and the statue of Heracles, the mythical founder of the city and deity linked to the Samnite world. The double rectangular enclosure, with a nearby sacred well situated in front of the steps leading up to the temple, can probably be identified as the tomb (heroon) of the hero, the mythical founder of the city. The **Samnite Palaestra** stands on the eastern side facing northwards. During the excavations, fragments were discovered of a marble statue of the so-called Doriphorus by Policletes, now kept in the Archaeological Museum of Naples. [m.g.]

Views of the
Triangular Forum

5 large theatre

6 gladiators' barracks

7 odeion

The Triangular Forum also led to the *Summa Cavea* of the Large Theatre of Pompeii which stood next to the *odeion* and the so-called Gladiators' Barracks which were once (2nd-1st century BC) the *porticus post scenam* of the theatre.

The **Large Theatre** was initially built in about the second century BC and was restored according to Roman taste during the colonial period (80 BC). The restoration work was carried out by the architect M. Artorius M. L. Primus (who signed his name, one of the very few occasions when there is a specific reference to an *architectus*). It can be seen at the entrance to the eastern access corridor. New features were introduced shortly after Pompeii was made a colony These included the change to the stage so that it followed

the Roman typology of theatre, the use of the awning (*velarium*) to provide shade during hot weather, the numbering of the seats and the memorial inscriptions in honour of several deceased notables of the city. Behind the stage of the theatre there was a large four-sided portico, surrounded by 74 Doric columns built of grey tuff from Nucera, which has been identified as a gymnasium.

The odeion or *teatrum tectum*, as it was known by the Romans, was built during the first few years of the colony (79 BC) at the instigation of the two duumvirs, probably as a meeting place for the two thousand colonists. Its function was similar to that of a *bouleuterion* (the Greek term for a council chamber). [*m.g.*]

Large theatre
cavea and view

8 house of menander

Like the House of the Gilded Cupids, this house belonged to Quintus Poppeus, a member of the Poppei family who were related to the empress Poppea Sabina.

The house is decorated in the Fourth Style. In the corner on the right there is a *lararium* in the form of a shrine.

The atrium leads into a room decorated with the epic cycle of the Illiad: *Cassandra*, *The Trojan Horse* and *Laocoon*, painted on an easel and then positioned within the fresco decoration in the Fourth Style (*picture excise*).

The garden is closed by plinths decorated with herons and hunting scenes. On the northern side there is a room (*oecus*) with a green background where the decoration is completed in the upper part by a frieze with the theme of the *Rape of the Lapith women by the Centaurs*. In the centre of the floor there is a mosaic portraying *Pygmies rowing a boat on the river Nile*. At the end of the garden there is a library, a domestic *sacellum* and a rectangular exhedra framed by two apsidal niches.

The central exhedra contains paintings of two seated poets: one is *Menander* who was identified by the archaeologist Amedeo Maiuri due to the verses that are still legible on the *rotulus* (roll of parchment) while the other is probably *Euripides*, providing a juxtaposition between tragedy and comedy. This can be seen from the theatrical masks portrayed on the small marble tables placed to the sides of the central deity, probably

Apollo. The apsidal exhedras are decorated with *Stories of Artemis and Aphrodite*.

The domestic sacellum contains a lararium on which there are casts of the wooden portraits of the ancestors (*imagines maiorum*). It is decorated in the Second Style with subsequent alterations.

There are reception rooms on the eastern side of the garden. In the centre there is a huge room (*oecus triclinare*) decorated in the First Style with decorated *cocciopesto* floors. The room was created above the

Lararium
atrium

The poet Menander
Central exedra

on the following pages
Lararium with plaster casts
of the wooden portraits
of the ancestors
household sacellum

Caldarium
Baths district

previous second century BC houses which were visible during the excavation. The adjacent room contains the skeletons of several farmers who died trying to plunder the houses after the eruption.

The house has a small but well-equipped spa area decorated with exotic caricatural silhouettes in the *apodyterium* (changing room) and mosaics with erotic scenes in the area between the warm and cold rooms. A corridor to the south leads to the agricultural area. The stables (*equile*) have a reconstruction of a farm wagon (only the iron and bronze parts are original).

A chest with 118 pieces of silverware, weighing 24 kilos, was hidden in the basement of the house. The silverware is now on display in the Archaeological Museum of Naples. Of the roughly five hundred silver vases scattered worldwide, almost half come from Pompeii. The Vesuvian villas are the only ancient villas to have yielded silverware services that were actually used. The services consisted of four similar pieces or multiples of four, according to the traditions of Roman dining. [*m.g.*]

Rape of Cassandra
Decoration in Fourth Style

Pygmies on the Nile
Detail of the mosaic floor
of the caldarium

on the previous pages
View of the atrium

View of the peristyle

Decoration of the peristyle
Internal plinth with plant
motif decoration, detail

9 house of the cryptoporticus

In 1911 Vittorio Spinazzola, the then director of archaeological works, decided to complete the excavations in Via dell'Abbondanza which had begun in the late nineteenth century but had been interrupted. His initiative led to the discovery of elegant residences such as this one which was named the House of the Cryptoporticus.

The bombing of Pompeii in 1943 caused significant damage to the eastern side of the building, causing the destruction of four rooms. The house was originally linked to the adjacent House of the Trojan Sacellum from which it was divided following the earthquake in 62 AD, appropriating the area occupied by the cryptoporticus. When the eruption took place in 79 AD, extensive restoration work was being carried out on the building as a result of earthquakes that had struck the city prior to

the final cataclysmic event. Evidence for this includes the unfinished decoration in the rooms near the entrance.

The long corridor that begins from the entrance at no.2 leads to the atrium which provides access to the peristyle. On the western side of the peristyle there is a *lararium* (shrine for the household gods) with Fourth Style decoration portraying *Hermes* in a niche with the serpent *Agathodaimon* (a good spirit) and a peacock.

From the peristyle (12) two staircases lead to rooms and other parts of the house. The main staircase leads to an upper loggia overlooking the garden, with a roofed summer triclinium (16) or dining room. The room contains masonry couches and a table with decoration on a red background with plants and birds in the base and a small adjoining kitchen. The other staircase leads to the cryptoporticus below, originally decorated in the Second Style with alternating herms of

Satyrs and Maenads and a continuous upper frieze with Trojan scenes and the names of the characters written in Greek. The various building phases of the cryptoporticus encapsulate the complex architectural history of the house. Together with the rectangular room (17) above, the cryptoporticus was once part of the House of the Trojan Sacellum although it was separated after the earthquake in 62 AD.

Its original function as an open portico overlooking the garden changed when the openings were walled up and the level of the garden was raised. A series of splayed windows were added along the northern, eastern and western sides and it acquired a new function as a cellar on the north wing.

The spa complex on the eastern side of the house, which dates to the Republican period and is contemporary with the original portico, was decorated in the Second Style with splendid mosaics and wall decoration. It is worth admiring the decoration of the *frigidarium* (20), with splendid theatrical stage sets that lead to landscapes and panoramas with dionysian themes and scenes of daily life with winged genii placed above. The most important discovery during the excavation of the house took place when a group of ten individuals were found. The men and women were of different social status and one individual, wearing iron rings around the ankles (*compedes*), has been identified as a slave. They were trying

to escape from the garden area, already covered in ash, and were caught by surprise by the advancing cloud of incandescent material. They had sought refuge in the wings of the cryptoporticus, waiting for the eruption to end, in the hope of making their escape by protecting themselves under the roof tiles from the showers of pumice. [*m.g.*]

on the previous pages
Atrium and impluvium

Hermes with the serpent
Agathodaimon and peacock
lararium

Frigidarium
View of the whole area

Caldarium
Detail of the mosaic floor

on the following pages
View of the cryptoporticus

10 fullonica of stephanus

During the excavations carried out in Via dell'Abbondanza during 1908/9, a skeleton with a hoard of coins was found in the entrance to a *fullonica* (laundry). The skeleton has been identified as Stephanus, the owner of the laundry whose name is known from the electoral inscriptions on the building, who was caught by surprise by the eruption of 79 AD.

Stephanus had transformed an old atrium house into a "modern" production unit which, besides being a place for washing clothes, was also used for degreasing new fabrics.

In the centre of the atrium there is a large tub instead of an *impluvium*, while other tubs are situated in the garden in the area behind the house and were used for productive purposes. The laundry (*fullonica*) was one of the wealthiest in the city. The main activities included washing, removing stains, redyeing and ironing used fabrics. It was also equipped with a wooden press (*pressorium*) for ironing clothes, situated on the eastern side of the entrance. The only surviving traces are the gaps left for fixing the press to the wall and the plaster cast made of a part of the machinery.

The room (g) was decorated with elegant Fourth Style paintings on a red background with figures portraying *The rapid succession of the seasons* in the central panels. The area that had once been a peristyle was also radically transformed by installing interconnected basins placed at different heights. The oval tubs were used for pounding the clothes (*saltus fullonici*), a task performed by workmen who stood in a mixture of water and soda or in diluted urine. The nearby steps led up to terraces where the fabrics were hung up to dry.

The painted pilaster with scenes of washing from the Fullonica of Veranius Hypseus (VI 8, 20), now in the National Archaeological Museum in Naples (inv. 9774), helps to

reveal the various tasks carried out by the corporation of the *fullones* (laundry workers): these include carding, in which a piece of fabric hung up on a pole is being carded with a brush, and sulphuring with a small bucket containing lit sulphur and a wicker basket, surmounted by the protective figure of an owl, on which the fabric was laid out. In the lower register, the workers tread on fabrics immersed in the tubs. On the adjoining side of the pilaster, the upper register features a painting of a wooden press which is identical to the one found in the *fullonica* of Stephanus. [*m.g.*]

Flying female figure
Detail of Fourth Style
decoration

View of room overlooking
atrium

on the following pages
Atrium with pool

basins for dyeing

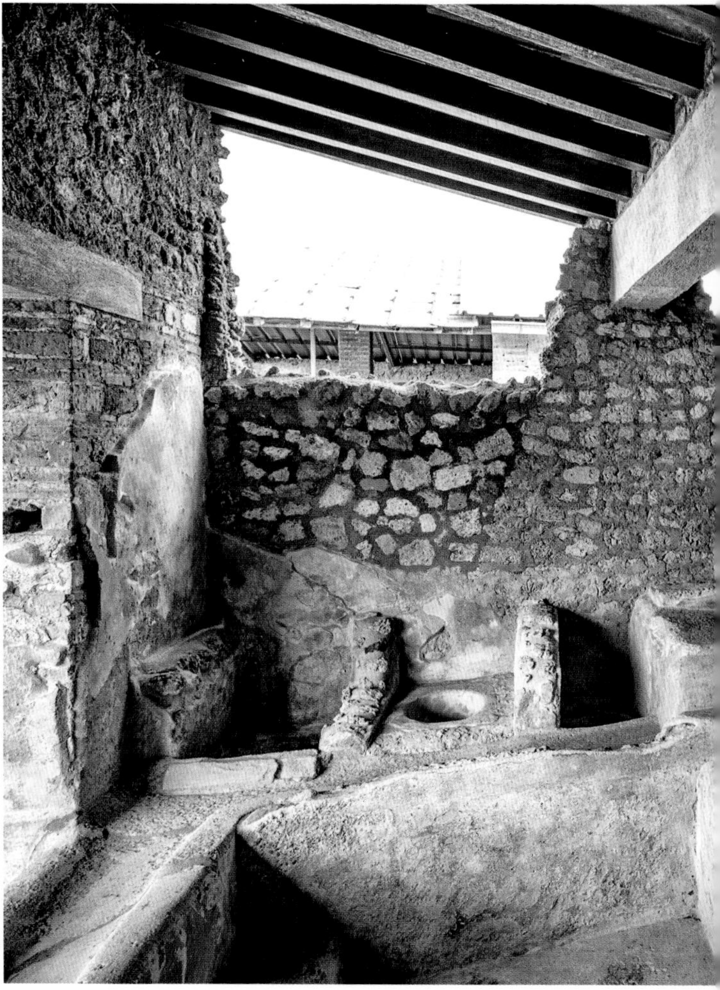

11 | house of paquius proculus

The house has generally been attributed to the baker (*pistor*) Paquius Proculus who became duumvir (magistrate) of Pompeii, as indicated by the copious amount of electoral propaganda on the outer façade of the house covered in electoral slogans.

The structure would have originally included an adjacent house to the west, as shown by openings that were walled up during a subsequent phase (first century BC) when the layout of the residence revolved around the creation of a garden and its rooms.

The floor visible from the atrium is a mosaic carpet with geometric images, portraits and animals. The image at the entrance shows a dog tied to a door while in the atrium the mosaic is subdivided into panels with animals.

The elegant rooms and bedrooms, decorated in the Third and Fourth Style, look onto the garden at the end created above an imposing cryptoporticus which was required to compensate for the difference in height of this part of the city. The cryptoporticus was also designed according to the layout of the cisterns which were used for draining and collecting rainwater.

It is worth mentioning the decoration of the triclinium (18) which has a central carpet mosaic with theatrical masks. The elegant adjacent room (*oecus*, 16) preserves restrained Third Style decoration on the walls and an unusual emblem in *vermiculatum* in the floor with an exotic Egyptianising theme: pygmies fishing in the river Nile

teeming with fish, birds and hippopotami, extremely similar to the mosaic in the triclinium (11) of the House of Menander. The skeletons of seven boys were found in the exhedra. [*m.g.*]

on previous pages
View of the atrium

Atrium
Details of the mosaic decoration

Entrance
Dog on a chain

Oecus
Detail of the emblem in the
floor with scene of pygmies
fishing on the nile

Atrium
Detail of the mosaic floor
with peacock

12 the house of the ephebe

The house takes its name from the discovery of a bronze statue of an *Ephebe* (Youth) as a lamp-bearer (now in the National archaeological Museum in Naples, inv. 143753). The statue was found wrapped in linen cloth and arranged together with other bronze statues of varying size in a series of rooms such as room (13), room (17) and the cubicle (11); dating to the Augustan period, the statue was gilded after it became part of the family treasure. The structure of the house was the result of a series of purchases, made over a period of time, of three terraced houses occupying the area of the *insula* (block). This is why the house has a double entrance and a double atrium; the first entrance at number (10), renovated in the second century BC with the addition of an upper floor, still seems to closed by the plaster cast that shows the original lock of the door, while the main entrance was at number (11).

The last owner may have been P. Cornelius Tages, a wine merchant whose name appears in electoral inscriptions in the nearby area.

The atrium in house no. (11), with a series of rooms decorated in the Fourth Style and a fragment of obsidian embedded in the eastern wall, leads to a large triclinium (17). The room is decorated in the Fourth Style on a white background with central paintings with a mythological themes such as *Helen and Menelaus* on the eastern side. There is also a floor in *opus sectile* with an

emblema (central panel) decorated with kaleidoscopic rosettes and lotus flowers made of glass paste and exotic marble.

On the western side of the external portico there is a painted lararium with a stuccoed niche and a Fourth Style fresco portraying *Mars and Venus with Eros*.

The garden has a summer triclinium with a fountain in the middle placed on the southern end wall. The masonry couches have ornate Fourth Style decoration on the base with images inspired by Egyptian themes and Nilotic scenes with temples, cities, statues and scenes of everyday life which could be viewed in perspective in the water from the fountain. [*m.g.*]

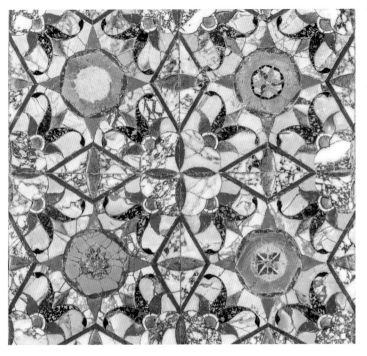

Mars and Venus
Fourth Style in the garden

Emblem
Floor of the triclinium

on the following pages
View of the entrance

View of the summer
triclinium

13 house of giulius polybius

The House of Giulius Polybius, which is open on Via dell'Abbondanza, has an imposing façade decorated in the First Style with tapering doors and a dentil cornice above the architrave. It was almost completely reconstructed after being damaged during the Second World War. A short poem scratched on the wall was found next to the fourth entrance: *Nothing can last forever/ Once the sun has shone, it returns beneath the sea/The moon, once full, wanes and [so] the wounds of love become a light breeze*.

The residence departs from the canons of the Pompeian house: it had two atriums, one entirely roofed and another with a *compluvium* and without columns (Tuscanic atrium).

The decoration was done in the First, Second, Third and Fourth styles, indicating that it was inhabited continuously for a long period.

The decoration of the black room at the end of the garden is particularly elegant and portrays the *Punishment of Dirce* in the Third Style.

At the time of the eruption, the building was still undergoing restoration due to the damage caused by the earthquakes which had affected the Pompeian areas since 62/63 AD, as reflected by a heap of lime in the first atrium.

Due to the restoration work, a collection of bronzes were kept in a special room just before the eruption: they included a statue of a young lamp-holder (*lampadophóros*), similar to the Apollo of Piombino, and a Laconian crater with a Greek inscription on the rim and a painting portraying *The Seven against Thebes*.

The skill displayed by the architectural decoration, which imitates the majestic Hellenistic palaces, is confirmed by the presence of a painted door. It is a typically Hellenistic door, tapering at the top, with bands decorated with studs and panels. Each of the upper panels has a painted figure.

The peristyle had wooden cupboards, as can be seen from the plaster casts made during the excavation, containing elegant glass furnishings, a complete pharmacopea (with lists of medicines and cures) and the owner's signet ring. The plaster casts made in the cavities of the roots have led to the identification of the original vegetation: an olive tree, a pear tree, a fig tree and climbing plants on the western side.

During the excavation thirteen skeletons were found. The victims, who may have been related, include an elderly man, two people holding hands and a pregnant woman. The owner of the mansion has been identified as Gaius Julius Polybius referred to in the electoral propaganda written in red on the façade and inside the house. [*m.g.*]

View of the exterior

Kitchen
Detail of the decoration

14 house of the orchard

The house is also known as the House of the Floral Cubicles due to the presence of two splendid cubicles decorated in Third Style. A cubicle with a sky blue background (8) overlooks the atrium while the other one with a black background (12), situated in the inner peristyle, is decorated with garden themes and is full of objects (*aegyptiaca*) related to Egyptianising cults.

The house, which originally had a Samnite layout with a Tuscanic atrium, was modernised and elaboratedly decorated in Third Style by an excellent workshop of painters that specialised in portraying *paradiseia* (imaginary gardens). The workshop was active in Pompeii during the Augustan period and also painted the same theme in the House of the Golden Bracelet.

The sky blue cubicle (8) is designed as a white pergola immersed in a garden full of bushes and trees such as bay, myrtle, oleander, palm, lemon, cherry and mountain strawberry tree (arbetus unedo). Birds in flight, such as blackbirds, magpies, swallows, swifts and turtle doves, are depicted everywhere. Slender vases on the pergola are surmounted by funerary urns and two paintings portraying the bull Apis with a solar disc between the horns and the key of life (*ankh*) hanging from the animal's neck. Two other paintings portray offering scenes. Two wreaths separated by theatrical masks and marble discs (*oscilla*) hang from the stucco cornice.

In the side panels, hidden among the vegetation, there are two Egyptian statues. The white marble statues, in a rigid pose, are either seated or stand on pedestals. They wear a headdress with a cobra (*ureus*), and have a sceptre and an *ankh*. In the central panels the garden is decorated with small paintings portraying dionysian themes.

In the wall decoration of the black cubicle (12), in line with the peristyle, the eastern wall portrays a serpent coiling itself around the trunk of a fig tree situated at the centre of a large garden with trees such as plum, lemon, strawberry tree, service tree and pear. The fence of the garden is made of trellis-

work. Inside the garden there are liturgical objects associated with Isiac cults such as several marble vases and a gold water jug (*hydria*) adorned with inset gems, with a long spout and a cobra-shaped handle; the vase rests on a wreath of rose leaves contained within a splendid marble support with plant motifs. The *hydria*, often portrayed in the hands of the offerers, contained the holy water of the Nile and was an object associated with the initiates.

The ceiling is decorated with a painting of a rose-covered pergola. Bacchus is portrayed in the centre of the scene. The god is shown riding a panther, surrounded by dionysian attributes such as theatrical masks, musical instruments, *oscilla* and drinking horns (*rhyta*) hanging from vines as well as flying cherubs (erotes). [*m.g.*]

Garden
detail of Third Style
decoration

on page 137
Serpent on the trunk
of a fig tree
detail of Third Style
decoration

15 house of octavius quartio

Although it was initially thought to belong to Loreius Tiburtinus, it was actually the property of Decimus Octavius Quartio at the moment of the eruption. This is shown by the discovery of a bronze seal with the name of the last owner, found in one of the rooms adjoining the atrium. The architecture was based on models used on a wider scale in the imperial villas, adapted here to the whole area of the block (*insula*).

The house has a tripartite residential area, including an atrium with a central fountain and two areas situated at different heights behind it with two water channels arranged perpendicular to each other.

To the sides of the Samnite entrance there are plaster casts of the original locking system of the large main door with bronze bosses. The entrance leads into the atrium with a flower-box surrounding the *impluvium* with rooms arranged around it decorated in the Fourth Style.

The *pars publica* (public sphere) of the house led to the private area through a small garden surrounded by a portico, around which there were reception rooms. A marble statue of an *ibis*, and statues of *Bes* and other Egyptian deities made of glazed terracotta and marble, were found in this area.

The large *oecus* (g), which overlooks a *viridarium*, has splendid Fourth Style decoration below the ceiling, with shells and stucco. The side walls have a high base with painted faux marble slabs and are decorated in the

upper part with two friezes with figures.

The lower frieze, which is smaller, illustrates the mythical premise to the Greek expedition against Troy, portraying the *Funeral games in honour of Patroclus* and *Achilles welcoming Priam into his tent*. Each scene is accompanied by captions in Latin.

The upper register depicts the *Expedition of Heracles against Laomedon, King of Troy*, in the form of a continually moving account, clearly of Hellenistic origin.

The large *oecus* (g) leads to the first of two porticoes with pergolas, one running east-west, at right angles to the larger portico which runs north-south. Both are adorned with fountains and an elegant combination

of sculptures and decorations in the Fourth Style on the walls.

At the centre of the large upper terrace running east-west (i) there was a canal (*euripus*), crossed by two bridge-like features with statuettes of fighting animals along the sides - the personification of a river, almost certainly the Nile – and a Muse, placed in the spaces between the pilasters.

At the eastern edge of the canal there was a biclinium with a fountain in the form of a an aedicula-type shrine. The interior of the shrine was decorated as a faux cave with a statuette of a Silenus from which water gushed forth. The lateral walls were decorated in Fourth Style with paintings portraying *Narcissus* and *Pyramus and Thisbe* with a rare signature of Lucius, a figure painter or *pictor*

imaginarius (*Lucius pinxit:* painted by Lucius). At the western edge there was an elegant reception room with a panel in the centre depicting a priest of Isis (*linigerus calvus*).

The lower terrace (l), running north-south, consisted of a large garden with a pergola situated to the sides of the central *euripus* with fountains and water features. The second canal, which is over fifty metres long, lies at right angles to the canal of the upper terrace and is linked to it by a nympheum in the form of a cave. The canal was decorated with fountains and niches with statues. A statue of a sleeping hermaphrodite was found in the garden close to the southern exit. [*m.g.*]

View of the garden

Room
detail of Fourth Style
decoration

Terrace

on the following pages
Narcissus
Pyramus and Thisbe
Fourth Style decoration
of the biclinium

on previous pages
Room
detail of Fourth Style
decoration

16 house of venus in the shell

The house, whose entrance lies along Via dell'Abbondanza, was damaged by bombing in 1943 and was only excavated in 1952. The original Samnite layout, traces of which survive in the imposing entrance and the atrium, was transformed after the earthquake in 62 AD by replacing the standard tablinium wtth a new peristyle.

The imposing reconstruction work and the new decoration of the rooms in the Fourth Style are also reflected by the enlargement of the atrium area at the expense of the adjoining house through the purchase of rooms to create a large *oecus* (18). The layout was commissioned by the family of the new owners (M. Satrius and D. Lucretius (Satrius) Valens) who are known from the electoral inscriptions in the nearby area.

The end wall of the peristyle is painted with the scene of *Venus emerging from a shell*, like a pearl, surrounded by cherubs. The goddess' hairstyle is done according to the fashion of the Neronian period. The naked figure of Venus is clumsily painted. This can be seen, for example, from the awkward perspective of the legs of the goddess even though the painting does have a theatrical effect if viewed from a certain distance. She has a fan in her right hand while, in her left hand, she holds a veil fluttering in the wind. Her divine nudity is enhanced by the presence of gold jewellery: a diadem, a necklace, bracelets on her wrists and ankles. The appearance of the goddess of beauty is juxtaposed with the figure of Mars, portrayed in statuesque form placed on a pedestal and marble basins with doves (the birds sacred to Venus) within a painted garden. The decoration of panels and faux tapestries takes no account of real architecture. Indeed, the main aim of the painters was not to subordinate the decorative scheme to architectural forms but to use it to open up the perimeter walls, in terms of perspective and illusion, to portray ideal and imaginary views.

The building was still undergoing restoration due to the damage caused by the earthquake of 62 AD and subsequent tremors, as can be seen by a room which had been plastered but was still unpainted. [*m.g.*]

Mars

Garden

The birth of Venus
Details of the Fourth Style
decoration of the peristyle

17 amphitheatre
18 large palaestra

The amphitheatre of Pompeii is the oldest known example from the Roman world together with the amphitheatre in Nola. It was constructed after the city was made a colony (80 BC) at the instigation of the first duumvirs C.Q. Valgus and M. Porcius who also built the Odeion. The amphitheatre was built in a peripheral part of the city close to the walls, partly to avoid disturbing the daily life of the city during the games.

Monumental triangular staircases led up to the *cavea* (tiered seating) with seats for the spectators. It could hold up to 20,000 spectators from all over Pompeii, the outskirts and nearby towns. The level of the arena was lower than the external area since part of the building was raised while part was embedded in the ground.

Gladiatorial games, which involved fights between men and animals (*venationes*) and between gladiators, used to take place within the arena. The games began with a solemn opening procession; the gladiators wore heavy completely decorated parade armour with helmets, daggers, shields and leg guards (most of these, now in the Archaeological Museum of Naples, were discovered behind the stage of the Large Theatre which had been turned into a gladiators' barracks during the final years of the city). In 59 AD the enthusiasm of the spectators boiled over into a violent clash between the inhabitants of Pompei and Nucera and

the episode was immortalised in a fresco now in the Archaeological Museum of Naples. Following the clashes, the Senate placed a ten-year "ban" on games in Pompeii but the measure was revoked in 62 AD following the powerful earthquake which struck the whole city.

The Large Palaestra, which is so-called to distinguish it from the Samnite Palaestra, stands in the large space surrounding the elliptical area of the amphitheatre. It consists of a large open square (about 140x140 metres) bounded by porticoes. Double rows of plane trees, of which plaster casts remain, were planted in the area. There is a pool (*natatio*, 23x35 metres) in the centre. The outer wall was surmounted by merlons and the side walls were covered in inscriptions faithfully reproduced in the wall decoration portraying the *Clash between the inhabitants of Nucera and Pompeii*.

It was built near the amphitheatre in the Augustan age both as a training ground for gladiators and as a meeting place for associations of young people (*Juventus Pompeiana*) to educate them in the imperial ideology. It provided the setting for processions on foot and horseback, simulations of battles, duels, discus throwing and jumping with weights.

The earthquake of 62 AD caused the entire wall on the northern side to collapse and evidence for this was discovered by Amedeo Maiuri during the excavations that began in 1931. Maiuri chose not to intervene to preserve evidence of the event but the wall was subsequently completely restored. [*m.g.*]

on pages 146/147
View of the amphitheatre

on pages 148/149
The large gymnasium viewed
from the amphitheatre

View of the large palaestra

19 fortifications and cemetery of porta nocera

Pompeii was surrounded by fortifications that stretched for 3.2 kilometres and ran round the entire edge of the plain. There were twelve defensive towers in the walls.

During the years 1813-1814 Joachim Murat, King of Naples, ordered a survey of the fortification walls to define the precise extent of the city. The city walls were largely brought to light by Amedeo Maiuri who removed the waste material from previous excavations within the city during lengthy work that lasted from 1959 to 1961.

The walls reflect the different building phases involved in the city's urban development. The first city wall-terrace was made in about the mid-sixth century BC using "pappamonte", a local grey-green tuff-like rock which can still be seen in several parts of the wall outside Porta Nocera.

In the first half of the fifth century BC the "pappamonte" wall was replaced with a double wall built of Sarno limestone, consisting of two parallel walls with a fill of rubble and compacted earth.

At the beginning of the Samnite period, between the late fourth and early third century BC, the inner wall was covered by an earthwork (*agger*), built directly against the outer wall, which also functioned in many stretches as a terracing wall.

In the third century BC a new double wall was built, this time with an earthwork behind it with various pipes to dispose of sewage from the city. Sarno limestone was used for the outer wall while grey Nucera tuff was used for the inner wall. These pipes (*speci*) were placed to the sides of the city

gates and ran parallel to the streets or the natural boundary of the plateau (Porta Occidentalis, Porta di Nola, Porta Stabia).

The last phase of work on the walls of Pompeii dates to the period 120-90 BC, shortly before the Social War, and featured the addition of sturdy watch towers, made of *opus incertum*, placed at regular intervals along the wall.

Like every ancient city, Pompeii's cemeteries were located outside the city gates. About 250 metres of the Porta Nocera cemetery, which extends along the street that runs in parallel from east to west, have been brought to light. A hundred yards away from the gate stands the funerary monument (*cippus*) of Titus Suedius Clemens, the imperial prefect who expropriated illegal structures built by private citizens on state property after the earthquake.

There are various types of tombs: tombs with a plinth surmounted by an altar, burial chambers with niches, mausoleums with one or more orders, shrines on plinths and, lastly, semi-circular benches (*schola*). Incineration was used as a funerary rite. [*m.g.*]

Porta Nocera

Tomb of Publius Flavius Philoxenus and Flavia Agathea

20 garden of the fugitives

The small house situated to the north of the block (*insula*) reflects the social features of this part of the city. The block consisted of *insulae* inhabited by the middle classes whose wealth came from specialist produce (wines, perfumed oils) which can be seen in large internal areas. The striking aspect of the house is the discovery of the bodies of an entire family,. The family consisted of masters and servants, although they cannot be distinguished from each other, who were about to escape from the layer of pumice which was already 3.5 metres high. However, the progress in single file of these men, women and children was brought to an abrupt halt by another pyroclastic flow which struck everyone, burying them in what appears to be an eternal sleep.

The excavations carried out by Amedeo Maiuri with the use of plaster casts reflected the final moments of an entire family who did not manage to escape the eruption of 79 AD. [*m.g.*]

Plaster casts of the victims
of the eruption
Garden of the fugitives